Always Wash Your Hands

By Eileen Rhonna Marita
Illustrated by Michael Magpantay

Library For All Ltd.

LIBRARY
FOR ALL

Library For All is an Australian not for profit organisation with a mission to make knowledge accessible to all via an innovative digital library solution. Visit us at libraryforall.org

Always Wash Your Hands

First published 2021

Published by Library For All Ltd
Email: info@libraryforall.org
URL: libraryforall.org

This book was made possible by the generous support of the Education Cooperation Program.

Original illustrations by Michael Magpantay

Always Wash Your Hands
Marita, Eileen Rhonna
ISBN: 978-1-922621-69-6
SKU01643

Always Wash
Your Hands

Always...

Wash your hands
after playing.

Wash your hands
after working.

Wash your hands
after using the toilet.

Wash your hands
before preparing food.

Wash your hands
before eating.

Wash your hands
after eating.

Wash your hands
after patting your pet.

Always remember to
wash your hands.

You can use these questions to talk about this book with your family, friends and teachers.

What did you learn from this book?

Describe this book in one word.
Funny? Scary? Colourful? Interesting?

How did this book make you feel when you finished reading it?

What was your favourite part of this book?

download our reader app
getlibraryforall.org

About the contributors

Library For All works with authors and illustrators from around the world to develop diverse, relevant, high quality stories for young readers. Visit libraryforall.org for the latest news on writers' workshop events, submission guidelines and other creative opportunities.

Did you enjoy this book?

We have hundreds more expertly curated original stories to choose from.

We work in partnership with authors, educators, cultural advisors, governments and NGOs to bring the joy of reading to children everywhere.

Did you know?

We create global impact in these fields by embracing the United Nations Sustainable Development Goals.

www.ingramcontent.com/pod-product-compliance
Lightning Source LLC
Chambersburg PA
CBHW040318050426
42452CB00018B/2908